Shirlee Finley

PLANT BASED DIET COOKBOOK

RECIPES FOR YOUR BREAKFAST

60 delicious, healthy and easy
recipes for your Plant Based Breakfast
that will help you stay fit and detox your body
while respecting nature

Table of Contents

BREAKFAST RECIPES

1. Cookie in a Mug

Preparation time: 5 minutes.

Cooking time: 2 minutes.

Servings: 1

Ingredients:

- 1 egg yolk
- 1 pinch cinnamon
- 1 pinch salt
- 1 tablespoon butter
- 1 tablespoon erythritol
- 1/8 teaspoon vanilla extract
- 2 tablespoons sugar-free chocolate chips
- 3 tablespoons almond flour

Directions:

1. In a microwave-safe mug or ramekin, melt butter in a microwave. Stir in cinnamon, salt, erythritol, and vanilla. Mix well. Add egg yolk and mix well.
2. Stir in almond flour. Mix well. Fold in chocolate chips. Press on the bottom of the mug or ramekin. On high, cook in a microwave for a minute and 10 seconds. Serve and enjoy!

Nutrition:

- **Calories:** 330
- **Protein:** 7.0g
- **Carbs:** 4.0g
- **Fat:** 31.0g

2. Vegan Fudgy Granola Bar

Preparation time: 15 minutes

Cooking time: 25 minutes

Servings: 16

Ingredients:

- 1 pinch salt
- 1(1/2) cups sliced almonds
- 1/2 cup flaked coconut (unsweetened)
- 1/2 cup pecans
- 1/2 cup sunflower seeds
- 1/2 cup dried, unsweetened cranberries (chopped)
- 1/2 cup butter
- 1/2 cup powdered erythritol
- 1/2 teaspoon vanilla extract

Directions:

1. With parchment paper, line a square baking dish and preheat the oven to 300°F. In a food processor, pulse sunflower seeds, pecans, coconut, and almonds until crumb-like.
2. In a bowl, add a pinch of salt and cranberries. Stir in crumb mixture and mix well. In a microwave-safe mug, melt butter in a 20-second interval. Whisk in vanilla extract and erythritol. Pour over granola crumbs and mix well.
3. Press mixture as compact as you can on a prepared dish. Pop in the oven and bake for 25 minutes. Let it cool and cut into 16 equal squares.

Nutrition:

- **Calories:** 180
- **Protein:** 4.0g
- **Carbs:** 5.0g
- **Fat:** 17.0g

3. Hummus Quesadillas

Preparation time: 5 minutes.

Cooking time: 15 minutes.

Servings: 1

Ingredients:

- 1 tortilla, whole wheat
- 1/4 cup diced roasted red peppers
- 1 cup baby spinach
- 1/3 teaspoon minced garlic
- ¼ teaspoon salt
- ¼ teaspoon ground black pepper
- 1/4 teaspoon olive oil
- 1/4 cup hummus
- Oil as needed

Directions:

1. Put your large pan on medium heat, add oil and when hot, add red peppers and garlic, season with salt and black pepper, and cook for 3 minutes until sauté.
2. Then stir in spinach, cook for 1 minute, remove the pan from heat and transfer the mixture to a bowl.
3. Prepare quesadilla and for this, spread hummus on one-half of the tortilla, then spread spinach mixture on it, cover the filling with the other half of the tortilla and cook in a pan for 3 minutes per side until browned. When done, cut the quesadilla into wedges and serve.

Nutrition:

- **Calories:** 187
- **Fat:** 9g
- **Carbs:** 16.3g
- **Protein:** 10.4g

4. Cinnamon Muffins

Preparation time: 15 minutes.

Cooking time: 15 minutes.

Servings: 12

Ingredients:

- 1 tablespoon cinnamon
- 1 teaspoon baking powder
- 1/2 cup almond flour
- 1/2 cup coconut oil
- 1/2 cup almond butter
- 1/2 cup pumpkin puree
- 2 scoops vanilla protein powder

Glaze ingredients:

- 1 tablespoon granulated sweetener of choice
- 2 teaspoons lemon juice
- 1/4 cup coconut butter
- 1/4 cup milk of choice

Directions:

1. Line 12 muffin tins with muffin liners and preheat the oven to 350°F. Whisk well cinnamon, baking powder, and protein powder in a medium bowl.
2. Whisk in coconut oil, almond butter, and pumpkin puree. Mix well. Evenly divide into prepared muffin tins.
3. Bake in the oven for 13 minutes or until cooked through. Move it to a wire rack and let it cool. Meanwhile, mix all glaze ingredients in a small bowl and drizzle over the cooled muffin.

Nutrition:

- **Calories:** 112
- **Protein:** 5.0g
- **Carbs:** 3.0g
- **Fat:** 9.0g

5. Fudgy Choco-Peanut Butter

Preparation time: 15 minutes.

Cooking time: 0 minutes.

Servings: 32

Ingredients:

- 4 ounces cream cheese (softened)
- 2 tablespoons unsweetened cocoa powder
- 1/2 cup butter
- 1/2 cup natural peanut butter
- 1/2 teaspoon vanilla extract
- 1/4 cup powdered erythritol

Directions:

1. In a microwave-safe bowl, mix peanut butter and butter. Microwave for 10-second interval until melted. While mixing every after sticking in the microwave.
2. Mix in vanilla extract, cocoa powder, erythritol, and cream cheese. Thoroughly mix. Line an 8x8-inch baking pan with foil and evenly spread mixture.
3. Place in the fridge to set and slice into 32 equal squares. Store in a tightly lidded container in the fridge and enjoy as a snack.

Nutrition:

- **Calories:** 65
- **Protein:** 1.5g
- **Carbs:** 1.0g
- **Fat:** 6.0g

6. Vegan Breakfast Biscuits

Preparation time: 10 minutes.

Cooking time: 10 minutes.

Servings: 6

Ingredients:

- 2 cups almond flour
- 1 tablespoon baking powder
- ¼ teaspoon salt
- ½ teaspoon onion powder
- ½ cup coconut milk
- ¼ cup nutritional yeast
- 2 tablespoons ground flaxseeds
- ¼ cup olive oil

Directions:

1. Preheat the oven to 450°F. Whisk together all the ingredients in a bowl. Divide the batter into a pre-greased muffin tin. Bake for 10 minutes.

Nutrition:

- **Calories:** 432
- **Fat:** 5g
- **Carbs:** 13g
- **Protein:** 8g

7. Scrumptious Ginger Cookies

Preparation time: 15 minutes.

Cooking time: 10 minutes.

Servings: 12

Ingredients:

- 1 teaspoon ground cinnamon
- 1 large organic egg
- 1/2 tablespoon ground ginger
- 1/4 teaspoon sea salt
- 3/4 cup coconut flour
- 3/4 cup unsalted butter (softened)
- 3/4 cup powdered brown sugar erythritol
- 1 1/2 cups almond flour

Directions:

1. Prepare 2 baking sheets lined using parchment paper and preheat the oven to 350°F. In a bowl, whisk well salt, cinnamon, ginger, coconut flour, and almond flour.

2. Add egg and beat well to mix. Knead until you form a dough. Scoop into balls. Roll in powdered erythritol.

3. Place in prepared baking sheet two inches apart. Flatten each cookie and bake until golden brown, around 9 minutes.

Nutrition:

- **Calories:** 190
- **Protein:** 3.5g
- **Carbs:** 5.5g
- **Fat:** 16.0g

8. Carrot Cake Balls

Preparation time: 15 minutes.

Cooking time: 0 minutes.

Servings: 15

Ingredients:

- 1/2 cup coconut flour
- 1/2 cup + 1 tablespoon water
- 2 tablespoons unsweetened applesauce
- 1/2 teaspoon vanilla extract
- 1 teaspoon cinnamon
- 4 tablespoons Lakanto Classic Monk Fruit Sweetener
- 1 medium carrot, finely chopped or shredded
- 4 tablespoons reduced-fat shredded coconut

Directions:

1. In a mixing bowl, whisk well vanilla extract, applesauce, water, and coconut flour. Stir in shredded carrots, Lakanto, and cinnamon. Mix well.
2. Place the dough in a fridge for 15 minutes. Place shredded coconut in a bowl. Evenly divide the dough into 15 equal parts and roll into balls.
3. Roll balls in a bowl of shredded coconut. Store in lidded containers and enjoy as a snack.

Nutrition:

- **Calories:** 24
- **Protein:** 1.0g
- **Carbs:** 3.0g
- **Fat:** 1.0g

9. Orange French Toast

Preparation time: 5 minutes.

Cooking time: 30 minutes.

Servings: 8

Ingredients:

- 2 cups of plant milk (unflavored)
- 4 tablespoons maple syrup
- 1(1/2) tablespoon cinnamon
- Salt (optional)
- 1 cup flour (almond)
- 1 tablespoon orange zest
- 8 bread slices

Directions:

1. Turn the oven and heat to 400°F afterward. In a cup, add the ingredients and whisk until the batter is smooth.
2. Dip each piece of bread into the paste and permit to soak for a couple of seconds. Put in the pan and cook until lightly browned.
3. Put the toast on the cookie sheet and bake for 10 to 15 minutes in the oven until it is crispy.

Nutrition:

- **Calories:** 129
- **Fat:** 1.1g
- **Carbs:** 21.5g
- **Protein:** 7.9g

10.Apple-Lemon Bowl

Preparation time: 15 minutes.

Cooking time: 0 minutes.

Servings: 1–2

Ingredients:

- 6 apples
- 3 tablespoons walnuts
- 7 dates
- 2 teaspoon Lemon juice
- 1/2 teaspoon cinnamon
- 2 Almonds
- 4 Seeds

Directions:

1. Root the apples, then break them into wide bits. In a food cup, put seeds, part of the lime juice, almonds, spices, and three-quarters of the apples.
2. Thinly slice until finely ground. Apply the remaining apples and lemon juice and make slices.

Nutrition:

- **Calories:** 249
- **Fat:** 5.1g
- **Carbohydrates:** 71.5g
- **Protein:** 7.9g

11. Coconut and Pineapple Pudding

Preparation time: 15 minutes.

Cooking time: 30 minutes.

Servings: 2

Ingredients:

- 2 tablespoons ground flaxseeds
- 2 cups unsweetened almond milk
- 1 tablespoon maple syrup
- ¼ cup chia seeds
- 1 teaspoon vanilla extract
- 2 tablespoons shredded, unsweetened coconut
- 1 Medjool date, pitted and chopped
- 2 cups sliced pineapple

Directions:

1. Put the flaxseeds, almond milk, maple syrup, chia seeds, and vanilla extract in a bowl. Stir to mix well.
2. Put the bowl in the refrigerator within 20 minutes, then remove it from the refrigerator and stir again. Place the bowl back to the refrigerator for 30 minutes or overnight to make the pudding.
3. Mix in the coconut and spread the date and pineapple on top before serving.

Nutrition:

- **Calories:** 513
- **Fat:** 22.9g
- **Carbs:** 66.4g
- **Protein:** 16.2g

12. Grilled Avocado with Tomatoes

Preparation time: 10 minutes.

Cooking time: 15 minutes.

Servings: 6

Ingredients:

- 3 avocados, halved and pitted
- 3 limes, wedged
- 1(½) cup grape tomatoes
- 1 cup fresh corn
- 1 cup onion, chopped
- 3 serrano peppers
- 2 garlic cloves, peeled
- ¼ cup cilantro leaves, chopped
- 1 tablespoon olive oil
- Salt and black pepper to taste

Directions:

1. Prepare and set a grill over medium heat.

2. Brush the avocado with oil and grill it for 5 minutes per side.
3. Meanwhile, toss the garlic, onion, corn, tomatoes, and pepper on a baking sheet.
4. At 550°F, roast the vegetables for 5 minutes.
5. Toss the veggie mix and stir in salt, cilantro, and black pepper.
6. Mix well, then fill the grilled avocadoes with the mixture.
7. Garnish with lime.
8. Serve.

Nutrition:

- **Calories:** 56
- **Total fat:** 6g
- **Carbs:** 3g
- **Net carbs:** 1g
- **Fiber:** 0g
- **Protein:** 1g

13.Banana Bites

Preparation time: 15 minutes.

Cooking time: 15 minutes.

Servings: 4

Ingredients:

- 2 bananas
- ½ cup vegan chocolate, melted
- 1 cup roasted pistachios, in pieces or finely crushed

Directions:

1. Set aside a parchment-lined baking sheet. Peel the bananas and stick a toothpick on both ends to make the next step easier.
2. Dip and fully coat the bananas in the melted chocolate. Set onto the parchment paper.
3. If using whole pistachios, place the nuts into a food processor and pulse until fine. Leave some pistachios intact.

4. Sprinkle the pistachios on top of the banana. Freeze the bananas to set the chocolate and pistachios for 5 minutes.
5. Remove the bananas and cut them into bites. Return to the freezer in a glass container. When ready to consume, remove bananas from the freezer and thaw for 10 minutes to soften.

Nutrition:

- **Calories** 273
- **Fat** 14g
- **Protein** 6g
- **Carbs** 37g

14.Chocolate Chip Coconut Pancakes

Preparation time: 5 minutes.

Cooking time: 30 minutes.

Servings: 8

Ingredients:

- 1(1/4) cup oats
- 2 teaspoons coconut flakes
- 2 cup plant milk
- 1(1/4) cup maple syrup
- 1(1/3) cup of chocolate chips
- 2(¼) cups buckwheat flour
- 2 teaspoons baking powder
- 1 teaspoon vanilla essence
- 2 teaspoons flaxseed meal
- Salt (optional)
- 1 teaspoon Sugar

Directions:

1. Put the flaxseed and cook over medium heat until the paste becomes a little moist. Remove seeds. Stir the buckwheat, oats, coconut chips, baking powder, and salt with each other in a wide dish.
2. In a large dish, stir together the retained flax water with the sugar, maple syrup, vanilla essence. Transfer the wet ingredients to the dry ingredients and shake to combine.
3. Place over medium heat the nonstick grill pan. Pour 1/4 cup flour into the grill pan with each pancake, and scatter gently. Cook for 5 to 6 minutes before the pancakes appear somewhat crispy.

Nutrition:

- **Calories:** 198
- **Fat:** 9.1g
- **Carbs:** 11.5g
- **Protein:** 7.9g

15.Avocado Pudding

Preparation time: 3 hours.

Cooking time: 0 minutes.

Servings: 4

Ingredients:

- 1 cup almond milk
- 2 avocados, peeled and pitted
- ¾ cup cocoa powder
- 1 teaspoon vanilla extract
- 2 tablespoons Stevia
- ¼ teaspoon cinnamon
- Walnuts, chopped for serving

Directions:

1. Add avocados to a blender and pulse well. Add cocoa powder, almond milk, Stevia, vanilla bean extract, and pulse the mixture well.
2. Pour into serving bowls and top with walnuts. Chill for 2–3 hours and serve!

Nutrition:

- **Calories:** 288
- **Carbs:** 34g
- **Fat:** 20g
- **Protein:** 4g

16.Sun-Butter Baked Oatmeal Cups

Preparation time: 10 minutes.

Cooking time: 25 minutes.

Servings: 12 cups.

Ingredients:

- 1/4 cup coconut sugar
- 1(1/2) rolled oats
- 2 tablespoons chia seeds
- 1/4 teaspoon salt
- 1 teaspoon cinnamon
- 1/2 cup non-dairy milk
- 1/2 cup Sun-Butter
- 1/2 cup applesauce

Directions:

1. Preheat the oven to 350°F. Mix all the ingredients and blend well. Add muffins and put extra toppings. Bake 25 minutes, or until golden brown.

Nutrition:

- **Calories:** 129
- **Fat:** 1.1g
- **Carbohydrates:** 1.5g
- **Protein:** 4.9g

17.Dairy-Free Coconut Yogurt

Preparation time: 5 minutes.

Cooking time: 0 minutes.

Servings: 2

Ingredients:

- 1 can coconut milk
- 4 vegan probiotic capsules

Directions:

1. Shake coconut milk with a whole tube. Remove the plastic capsules and mix in. Cut a 12-inch cheesecloth until stirred. Freeze or eat immediately.

Nutrition:

- **Calories:** 219
- **Fat:** 10.1g
- **Carbohydrates:** 1.5g
- **Protein:** 7.9g

18.Crusty Grilled Corn

Preparation time: 10 minutes.

Cooking time: 15 minutes.

Servings: 4

Ingredients:

- 2 corn cobs
- 1/3 cup Vegenaise
- 1 small handful cilantro
- ½ cup breadcrumbs
- 1 teaspoon lemon juice

Directions:

1. Preheat the gas grill on high heat.
2. Add corn grill to the grill and continue grilling until it turns golden-brown on all sides.
3. Mix the Vegenaise, cilantro, breadcrumbs, and lemon juice in a bowl.
4. Add grilled corn cobs to the crumbs mixture.
5. Toss well, then serve.

Nutrition:

- **Calories:** 253
- **Total fat:** 13g
- **Protein:** 31g
- **Total carbs:** 3g
- **Fiber:** 0g
- **Net carbs:** 3g

19.Strawberry Sushi

Preparation time: 15 minutes.

Cooking time: 25 minutes.

Servings: 24 sushi.

Ingredients:

- 3 cups cooked white sushi rice
- 3 tablespoons fresh lemon juice
- ½ teaspoon vanilla extract
- ½ cup maple sugar
- 2 cups strawberries, hulled and quartered
- 3 tablespoons chia seeds
- Salt to taste (optional)

Directions:

1. Combine the cooked sushi rice, lemon juice, vanilla extract, and maple sugar in a large bowl. Stir to mix well.
2. Wrap a sushi mat with plastic wrap, then arrange 1 cup of rice on top and press into ½-inch thick.
3. Arrange a row of strawberries on the rice and leave a 1-inch gap from the bottom side. Sprinkle with 1 teaspoon of chia seeds.
4. Use the plastic wrap and sushi mat to help to roll the rice into a cylinder. When you roll, pull the plastic wrap and sushi mat away from the rice at the same time. Repeat with the remaining rice and chia seeds.
5. Sprinkle the rolls with salt, if desired. Let stand for 5 minutes and slice each roll into 8 sushi. Serve immediately.

Nutrition:

- **Calories:** 295
- **Carbs:** 55g
- **Fat:** 6g
- **Protein:** 5g

20. Banana Waffles

Preparation time: 5 minutes.

Cooking time: 5 minutes.

Servings: 6

Ingredients:

- 1/4 teaspoon ground nutmeg
- 1 cup cashew milk, unsweetened
- 1 teaspoon ground cinnamon
- 2(1/2) tablespoon cashew butter
- 1/4 teaspoon baking soda
- 1 peeled medium banana
- 1 tablespoon baking powder
- 7 ounces all-purpose flour
- 2 tablespoons sugar

Directions:

1. In a blender, add all the ingredients on the list, cashew milk, and baking soda first. Blend for a minute until smooth.
2. In a waffle maker, use a spoon to transfer the mixture and cook the batter over medium-high heat. Your machine might not tell you when they are ready. Take them off when you can no longer see steam.

Nutrition:

- **Calories:** 200
- **Carbs:** 35g
- **Protein:** 4g
- **Fat:** 5g

21. Roasted Cashew and Almond Butter Delight

Preparation time: 5 minutes.

Cooking time: 12 minutes.

Servings: 1 & ½ cup.

Ingredients:

- 1 cup almonds, blanched
- 1/3 cup cashew nuts
- 2 tablespoons coconut oil
- Salt as needed
- ½ teaspoon cinnamon

Directions:

1. Preheat your oven to 350°F. Bake almonds and cashews for 12 minutes. Let them cool.
2. Move to a food processor and put the remaining ingredients. Add oil and keep blending until smooth. Serve and enjoy!

Nutrition:

- **Calories:** 205
- **Fat:** 19g
- **Protein:** 2.8g

22. Caramel Chia Seed Pudding

Preparation time: 10 minutes.

Cooking time: 0 minutes.

Servings: 4

Ingredients:

- 1 cup date caramel
- 2(1/8-ounces) chia seeds
- 2 tablespoons maple syrup
- 1 cup of coconut milk
- 1 teaspoon vanilla extract
- 1/4 cup water
- A pinch of salt

Directions:

1. In a blender, add coconut milk, chia seeds, salt, vanilla, maple syrup, and water. Properly blend this mixture until smooth.
2. Place the blended mixture into a sealed container and refrigerate for about 2 hours or overnight.
3. Get a jar and add the date caramel before the refrigerated coconut milk mixture. Do this for about 4 layers in one jar.

Nutrition:

- **Calories:** 316
- **Carbs:** 50g
- **Protein:** 4.4g
- **Fats:** 13g

23. Tasty Nut Packed Porridge

Preparation time: 10 minutes.

Cooking time: 15 minutes.

Servings: 4

Ingredients:

- 1 cup cashew nuts, raw and unsalted
- 1 cup pecans, halved
- 2 tablespoons Stevia
- 4 teaspoons coconut oil, melted
- 2 cups of water

Directions:

1. Slice the nuts in a food processor and form a smooth paste. Add water, oil, Stevia to the nut paste and transfer the mix to a saucepan.
2. Stir cook for 5 minutes on high heat. Reduce heat to low and simmer for 10 minutes. Serve warm and enjoy!

Nutrition:

- **Calories:** 260
- **Fat:** 22g
- **Carbohydrates:** 12g
- **Protein:** 6g

24. Greek Garbanzo Beans on Toast

Preparation time: 25 minutes.

Cooking time: 5 minutes.

Servings: 2

Ingredients:

- 2 tablespoons olive oil
- 3 small shallots, finely diced
- 2 large garlic cloves, finely diced
- ¼ teaspoon smoked paprika
- ½ teaspoon cinnamon
- ½ teaspoon salt
- ½–1 teaspoon sugar to taste
- Black pepper to taste
- 1 x 14ounces can peel plum tomatoes
- 2 cups cooked garbanzo beans
- 4–6 slices of crusty bread, toasted

Directions:

1. Pop a skillet over medium heat and add the oil. Add the shallots to the pan and cook for five minutes. Add the garlic and cook until ready, then add the other spices to the pan.
2. Stir well, then add the tomatoes. Lower the heat and simmer on low until the sauce thickens. Add the garbanzo beans and warm through. Season with sugar, salt, and pepper, then Serve and enjoy!

Nutrition:

- **Calories:** 709g
- **Fat:** 12g
- **Carbs:** 23g
- **Protein:** 19g

25. Ging Blueberry French Toast Breakfast Muffins

Preparation time: 20 minutes.

Cooking time: 25 minutes.

Servings: 12

Ingredients:

- 1 cup unsweetened plant milk
- 1 tablespoon ground flaxseed
- 1 tablespoon almond meal
- 1 tablespoon maple syrup
- 1 teaspoon vanilla extract
- 1 teaspoon cinnamon
- 2 teaspoons nutritional yeast
- ¾ cup frozen blueberries
- 9 slices soft bread
- ¼ cup oats
- 1/3 cup raw pecans
- ¼ cup of coconut sugar
- 3 tablespoons coconut butter, at room temperature
- 1/8 teaspoon sea salt
- 9 slices bread, each cut into 4

Directions:

1. Preheat your oven to 370°F and grease a muffin tin. Pop to one side. Find a medium bowl and add the flaxseeds, almond meal, nutritional yeast, maple syrup, milk, vanilla, and cinnamon.
2. Mix well using a fork, then pop into the fridge. Grab your food processor and add the topping ingredients (except the coconut butter.) Whizz to combine.
3. Add the butter, then whizz again. Grab your muffin tin and add a teaspoon of the flax and cinnamon batter to the bottom of each space.
4. Add a square of the bread, then top with 5–6 blueberries. Sprinkle with 2 teaspoons of the crumble, then top with another piece of bread.
5. Place 6 more blueberries over the bread, sprinkle with more of the topping, and then add the other piece of bread.
6. Add a tablespoon of the flax and cinnamon mixture on top and add a couple of blueberries on the top.
7. Pop into the oven and cook for 20–25 minutes until the top begins to brown. Serve and enjoy!

Nutrition:

- **Calories:** 132g
- **Fat:** 5g
- **Carbs:** 14g
- **Protein:** 3g

26. erbread Waffles

Preparation time: 30 minutes.

Cooking time: 20 minutes.

Servings: 6

Ingredients:

- 1 cup spelt flour
- 2 teaspoons baking powder
- ¼ teaspoon salt
- 1 tablespoon ground flaxseeds
- 1(½) teaspoon ground cinnamon
- 2 teaspoons ground ginger
- 4 tablespoons coconut sugar
- ¼ teaspoon baking soda
- 1(½) tablespoon olive oil
- 1 cup non-dairy milk
- 1 tablespoon apple cider vinegar
- 2 tablespoons blackstrap molasses

Directions:

1. Take a waffle iron, oil generously, and preheat. Take a large bowl and add the dry ingredients. Stir well together.
2. Put the wet ingredients into another bowl and stir until combined. Stir the dry and wet together until combined.
3. Pour the mixture into the waffle iron and cook at a medium temperature for 20 minutes. Open carefully and remove. Serve and enjoy!

Nutrition:

- **Calories:** 173
- **Fat:** 5g
- **Carbs:** 29g
- **Protein:** 3g

27. Oatmeal and Carrot Cake

Preparation time: 5 minutes.

Cooking time: 10 minutes.

Servings: 2

Ingredients:

- 1 cup of water
- ½ teaspoon of cinnamon
- 1 cup of rolled oats
- Salt to taste
- ¼ cup of raisins
- ½ cup of shredded carrots
- 1 cup of non-dairy milk
- ¼ teaspoon of allspice
- ½ teaspoon of vanilla extract

Toppings:

- ¼ cup of chopped walnuts
- 2 tablespoons of maple syrup
- 2 tablespoons of shredded coconut

Directions:

1. Put a small pot on low heat and bring the non-dairy milk, oats, and water to a simmer. Now, add the carrots, vanilla extract, raisins, salt, cinnamon, and allspice.
2. You need to simmer all the ingredients, but do not forget to stir them. You will know that they are ready when the liquid is fully absorbed into all the ingredients (in about 7–10 minutes).
3. Transfer the thickened dish to bowls. You can top them with coconut or walnuts. This nutritious bowl will allow you to start your day.

Nutrition:

- **Calories:** 210
- **Fat:** 11g
- **Carbs:** 42g
- **Protein:** 4g

28. Almond Butter Banana Overnight Oats

Preparation time: 5 minutes.

Cooking time: 10 minutes.

Servings: 2

Ingredients:

- ½ cup rolled oats
- 1 cup almond milk
- 1 tablespoon chia seeds
- ¼ teaspoon vanilla extract
- ½ teaspoon ground cinnamon
- 1 tablespoon honey or maple syrup
- 1 banana, sliced
- 2 tablespoons natural almond butter

Directions:

1. Put the oats, milk, chia seeds, vanilla, cinnamon, and honey in a large bowl. Stir to combine, then divide half of the mixture between two bowls.
2. Top with the banana and peanut butter, then add the remaining mixture. Cover then pop into the fridge overnight. Serve and enjoy!

Nutrition:

- **Calories:** 227
- **Fat:** 11g
- **Carbs:** 35g
- **Protein:** 7g

29. Peach & Chia Seed Breakfast Parfait

Preparation time: 5 minutes.

Cooking time: 10 minutes.

Servings: 4

Ingredients:

- ¼ cup chia seeds
- 1 tablespoon pure maple syrup
- 1 cup of coconut milk
- 1 teaspoon ground cinnamon
- 3 medium peaches, diced small
- 2/3 cup granola

Directions:

1. Find a small bowl and add the chia seeds, maple syrup, and coconut milk. Stir well, then cover and pop into the fridge for at least one hour.
2. Find another bowl, add the peaches and sprinkle with the cinnamon. Pop to one side. When it's time to serve, take two glasses, and pour the chia mixture between the two.
3. Sprinkle the granola over the top, keeping a tiny amount to one side to use to decorate later. Top with the peaches and the reserved granola and serve.

Nutrition:

- **Calories:** 260
- **Fat:** 13g
- **Carbs:** 22g
- **Protein:** 6g

30. Avocado Toast with White Beans

Preparation time: 5 minutes.

Cooking time: 6 minutes.

Servings: 4

Ingredients:

- ½ cup canned white beans, drained and rinsed
- 2 teaspoons tahini paste
- 2 teaspoons lemon juice
- ½ teaspoon salt
- ½ avocado, peeled and pit removed
- 4 slices whole-grain bread, toasted
- ½ cup grape tomatoes, cut in half

Directions:

1. Grab a small bowl and add the beans, tahini, ½ lemon juice, and ½ salt. Mash with a fork. Take another bowl and add the avocado and the remaining lemon juice and salt. Mash together.
2. Place your toast onto a flat surface and add the mashed beans, spreading well. Top with the avocado and the sliced tomatoes, then Serve and enjoy!

Nutrition:

- **Calories:** 140
- **Fat:** 5g
- **Carbs:** 13g
- **Protein:** 5g

31.Oatmeal & Peanut Butter Breakfast Bar

Preparation time: 10 minutes.

Cooking time: 0 minutes.

Servings: 8

Ingredients:

- 1(½) cups date, pit removed
- ½ cup peanut butter
- ½ cup old-fashioned rolled oats

Directions:

1. Grease a baking tin and pop to one side. Grab your food processor, add the dates, and whizz until chopped.
2. Add the peanut butter and the oats and pulse. Scoop into the baking tin, then pop into the fridge or freezer until set. Serve and enjoy!

Nutrition:

- **Calories:** 232
- **Fat:** 9g
- **Carbs:** 32g
- **Protein:** 8g

32. Chocolate Chip Banana Pancake

Preparation time: 15 minutes.

Cooking time: 3 minutes.

Servings: 6

Ingredients:

- 1 large ripe banana, mashed
- 2 tablespoons coconut sugar
- 3 tablespoons coconut oil, melted
- 1 cup of coconut milk
- 1(½) cups whole wheat flour
- 1 teaspoon baking soda
- ½ cup vegan chocolate chips
- Olive oil, for frying

Directions:

1. Grab a large bowl and add the banana, sugar, oil, and milk. Stir well. Add the flour and baking soda and stir again until combined.
2. Add the chocolate chips and fold through, then pop to one side. Put a skillet over medium heat and add a drop of oil.
3. Pour ¼ of the batter into the pan and move the pan to cover. Cook for 3 minutes, then flip and cook on the other side. Repeat with the remaining pancakes, then Serve and enjoy!

Nutrition:

- **Calories:** 105
- **Fat:** 13g
- **Carbs:** 23g
- **Protein:** 5g

33. Chia Seeds Pudding with Fruits

Preparation time: 5 minutes.

Cooking time: 0 minutes.

Servings: 2

Ingredients:

- 1 tablespoon ground flaxseed
- ¼ teaspoon ground cinnamon
- 1/8 teaspoon ground nutmeg
- 1–2 tablespoons pure maple syrup
- 1 tablespoon chia seeds
- ½ cup almond milk

Topping:

- 1 banana, sliced
- 1/2 cup fresh mango, cubes
- 1 tablespoon shredded coconut

Directions:

1. In a bowl, combine all the ingredients and mix well. Cover and place in the refrigerator overnight.
2. In the morning, stir the mixture and add some almond milk or water. For serving, set banana slice in a serving jar. Pour pudding in it. Top with mango cubes and coconut. Enjoy!

Nutrition:

- **Calories:** 420
- **Carbs:** 35g
- **Fat:** 30g
- **Protein:** 16g

34. Rice Pudding

Preparation time: 5 minutes.

Cooking time: 30 minutes.

Servings: 4

Ingredients:

- 1 can coconut milk
- 1/2 teaspoon ground cardamom
- 1/2 teaspoon cinnamon
- 2 tablespoons maple syrup
- 1(1/2) cups cooked brown rice
- 2 teaspoons orange zest

Topping:

- Fresh berries for topping
- ¼ cup chopped almonds

Directions

1. Heat nonstick pot over medium heat, add milk and cardamom. Cook it for one minute, then reduce heat to low and let simmer for 10 minutes.
2. Add the cinnamon and maple syrup and stir until combined. Add rice in the same pan and simmer on medium-low heat for 10 minutes until the rice is mixed with milk and is creamy.
3. Stir in the orange zest. Once cooked, remove from the heat—top rice pudding with fresh berries and nuts. Enjoy!

Nutrition:

- **Calories:** 232
- **Carbs:** 52g
- **Fat:** 2g
- **Protein:** 4g

35. Quinoa with Berries

Preparation time: 5 minutes.

Cooking time: 15 minutes.

Servings: 4

Ingredients:

- 2 cups almond milk
- 3/4 cups uncooked quinoa
- 1 tablespoon almond butter
- 3 chopped walnuts
- 1 tablespoon maple syrup
- 1 cup strawberries
- 1-ounce sunflower seeds

Directions:

1. Heat-up your nonstick pan over medium heat and pour milk into a saucepan. Boil milk, add quinoa, and reduce heat to medium.
2. Cover and simmer for 15 minutes or until the milk has been absorbed. Remove from the heat, add some milk, almond butter, walnuts, and maple syrup.
3. Stir, then put the quinoa in a bowl. Top with strawberries and sunflower seeds. Serve and enjoy!

Nutrition:

- **Calories:** 300
- **Carbs:** 40g
- **Fat:** 10g
- **Protein:** 13g

36. Oatmeal Breakfast Cookies

Preparation time: 15 minutes.

Cooking time: 12 minutes.

Servings: 5

Ingredients:

- 1 tablespoon ground flaxseed
- 2 tablespoons almond butter/sunflower seed butter
- 2 tablespoons maple syrup
- 1 banana, mashed
- 1 teaspoon ground cinnamon
- ¼ teaspoon ground nutmeg (optional)
- Pinch sea salt
- ½ cup rolled oats
- ¼ cup raisins, or dark chocolate chips

Directions:

1. Preheat the oven to 350°F. Prepare your large baking sheet lined with parchment paper. Mix the ground flax with just enough water to cover it in a small dish, and leave it to sit.
2. In a large bowl, mix the almond butter and maple syrup until creamy, then add the banana. Add the flax-water mixture.
3. Sift the cinnamon, nutmeg, and salt into a separate medium bowl, then stir into the wet mixture. Add the oats and raisins, and fold in.
4. Form 3 to 4 tablespoons of batter into a ball and press lightly to flatten onto the baking sheet. Repeat, spacing the cookies 2 to 3 inches apart.
5. Bake within 12 minutes, or until golden brown. Store the cookies in an airtight container in the fridge, or freeze them for later.

Nutrition:

- **Calories:** 192
- **Fat:** 6g
- **Carbs:** 34g
- **Protein:** 4g

37. Sunshine Muffins

Preparation time: 15 minutes.

Cooking time: 30 minutes.

Servings: 6

Ingredients:

- 1 teaspoon coconut oil for greasing muffin tins (optional)
- 2 tablespoons almond butter/sunflower seed butter
- ¼ cup non-dairy milk
- 1 orange, peeled
- 1 carrot, coarsely chopped
- 2 tablespoons chopped dried apricots/other dried fruit
- 3 tablespoons molasses
- 2 tablespoons ground flaxseed
- 1 teaspoon apple cider vinegar
- 1 teaspoon pure vanilla extract
- ½ teaspoon ground cinnamon
- ½ teaspoon ground ginger (optional)

- ¼ teaspoon ground nutmeg (optional)
- ¼ teaspoon allspice (optional)
- ¾ cup rolled oats or whole-grain flour
- 1 teaspoon baking powder
- ½ teaspoon baking soda

Mix-ins (optional):

- ½ cup rolled oats
- 2 tablespoons raisins or other chopped dried fruit
- 2 tablespoons sunflower seeds

Directions:

1. Preheat the oven to 350°F. Prepare a 6-cup muffin tin by rubbing the cups' insides with coconut oil or using silicone or paper muffin cups.
2. Purée the nut butter, milk, orange, carrot, apricots, molasses, flaxseed, vinegar, vanilla, cinnamon, ginger, nutmeg, and allspice in a food processor or blender until somewhat smooth.
3. Grind the oats in a clean coffee grinder until they're consistent with flour (or use whole-grain flour). In a

large bowl, mix the oats with the baking powder and baking soda.

4. Mix the wet ingredients into the dry ingredients until just combined. Fold in the mix-ins (if using).
5. Spoon about ¼ cup batter into each muffin cup and bake for 30 minutes, or until a toothpick inserted into the center comes out clean.

Nutrition:

- **Calories:** 287
- **Fat:** 12g
- **Carbs:** 41g
- **Protein:** 8g

38. Applesauce Crumble Muffins

Preparation time: 15 minutes.

Cooking time: 15–20 minutes.

Servings: 12

Ingredients:

- 1 teaspoon coconut oil for greasing muffin tins (optional)
- 2 tablespoons nut butter or seed butter
- 1½ cups unsweetened applesauce
- 1/3 cup coconut sugar
- ½ cup non-dairy milk
- 2 tablespoons ground flaxseed
- 1 teaspoon apple cider vinegar
- 1 teaspoon pure vanilla extract
- 2 cups whole-grain flour
- 1 teaspoon baking soda
- ½ teaspoon baking powder
- 1 teaspoon ground cinnamon
- Pinch sea salt
- ½ cup walnuts, chopped

Toppings (optional):

- ¼ cup walnuts
- ¼ cup of coconut sugar
- ½ teaspoon ground cinnamon

Directions:

1. Preheat the oven to 350°F. Prepare two 6-cup muffin tins by rubbing the cups' insides with coconut oil or using silicone or paper muffin cups.
2. In a large bowl, mix the nut butter, applesauce, coconut sugar, milk, flaxseed, vinegar, and vanilla until thoroughly combined, or purée in a food processor or blender.
3. In another large bowl, sift together the flour, baking soda, baking powder, cinnamon, salt, and chopped walnuts. Mix the dry ingredients into the wet ingredients until just combined.
4. Spoon about ¼ cup batter into each muffin cup and sprinkle with the topping of your choice (if using). Bake for 15 to 20 minutes, or until a toothpick inserted into the center comes out clean.

Nutrition:

- **Calories:** 287
- **Fat:** 12g
- **Carbs:** 41g
- **Protein:** 8g

39. Cinnamon Apple Toast

Preparation time: 5 minutes.

Cooking time: 10–20 minutes.

Servings: 12

Ingredients:

- 1 to 2 teaspoons coconut oil
- ½ teaspoon ground cinnamon
- 1 tablespoon maple syrup or coconut sugar
- 1 apple, cored and thinly sliced
- 2 slices whole-grain bread

Directions:

1. In a large bowl, mix the coconut oil, cinnamon, and maple syrup. Add the apple slices and toss with your hands to coat them.
2. To panfry the toast, place the apple slices in a medium skillet on medium-high and cook for about 5 minutes, or until slightly soft, then transfer to a plate.

3. Cook the bread in the same skillet for 2 to 3 minutes on each side. Top the toast with the apples. Alternately, you can bake the toast.
4. Use your hands to rub each slice of bread with some of the coconut oil mixtures on both sides. Lay them on a small baking sheet, top with the coated apples.

Nutrition:

- **Calories:** 187
- **Fat:** 8g
- **Carbs:** 27g
- **Protein:** 4g

40. Muesli and Berries Bowl

Preparation time: 10 minutes.

Cooking time: 0 minutes.

Servings: 5

Ingredients:

For the muesli:

- 1 cup rolled oats
- 1 cup spelt flakes, or quinoa flakes, or more rolled oats
- 2 cups puffed cereal
- ¼ cup sunflower seeds
- ¼ cup almonds
- ¼ cup raisins
- ¼ cup dried cranberries
- ¼ cup chopped dried figs
- ¼ cup unsweetened shredded coconut
- ¼ cup non-dairy chocolate chips
- 1 to 3 teaspoons ground cinnamon

For the bowl:

- ½ cup non-dairy milk, or unsweetened applesauce
- ¾ cup muesli
- ½ cup berries

Directions:

1. Put the muesli ingredients in a container or bag and shake. Combine the muesli and bowl ingredients in a bowl or to-go container.

Nutrition:

- **Calories:** 441
- **Fat:** 20g
- **Carbs:** 63g
- **Protein:** 10g

41.Chocolate Quinoa Breakfast Bowl

Preparation time: 5 minutes.

Cooking time: 30 minutes.

Servings: 2

Ingredients:

- 1 cup quinoa
- 1 teaspoon ground cinnamon
- 1 cup non-dairy milk
- 1 cup of water
- 1 large banana
- 2 to 3 tablespoons unsweetened cocoa powder or carob
- 1 to 2 tablespoons almond butter or other nut or seed butter
- 1 tablespoon ground flaxseed, or chia or hemp seeds
- 2 tablespoons walnuts
- ¼ cup raspberries

Directions:

1. Put the quinoa, cinnamon, milk, and water in a medium pot. Bring to a boil over high heat, then turn down low and simmer, covered, for 25 to 30 minutes.
2. While the quinoa is simmering, purée or mash the banana in a medium bowl and stir in the cocoa powder, almond butter, and flaxseed.
3. To serve, spoon 1 cup cooked quinoa into a bowl, top with half the pudding and half the walnuts and raspberries.

Nutrition:

- **Calories:** 392
- **Fat:** 19g
- **Carbs:** 49g
- **Protein:** 12g

42. Fruity Granola

Preparation time: 15 minutes.

Cooking time: 45 minutes.

Servings: 5 cups.

Ingredients:

- 2 cups rolled oats
- ¾ cup whole-grain flour
- 1 tablespoon ground cinnamon
- 1 teaspoon ground ginger (optional)
- ½ cup sunflower seeds, or walnuts, chopped
- ½ cup almonds, chopped
- ½ cup pumpkin seeds
- ½ cup unsweetened shredded coconut
- 1¼ cups pure fruit juice (cranberry, apple, or something similar)
- ½ cup raisins, or dried cranberries
- ½ cup Goji berries (optional)

Directions:

1. Preheat the oven to 350°F. Mix the oats, flour, cinnamon, ginger, sunflower seeds, almonds, pumpkin seeds, and coconut in a large bowl.
2. Sprinkle the juice over the batter, then mix until it's just moistened.
3. Spread the granola on a large baking sheet (the more spread out it is, the better), and put it in the oven. After about 15 minutes, use a spatula to turn the granola so that the middle gets dried out.
4. Let the granola bake until it's as crunchy as you want it, about 30 minutes more. Remove the granola and stir in the raisins and Goji berries (if using). Serve.

Nutrition:

- **Calories:** 398
- **Fat:** 25g
- **Carbs:** 39g
- **Protein:** 11g

43. Apple Porridge

Preparation time: 10 minutes.

Cooking time: 5 minutes.

Servings: 2

Ingredients:

- 1 large apple, peeled, cored, and grated
- 1 cup unsweetened almond milk
- 1(½) tablespoon of sunflower seeds
- 1/8 cup of fresh blueberries
- ¼ teaspoon of fresh vanilla bean extract

Directions:

1. Take a large pan and add sunflower seeds, vanilla extract, almond milk, apples, and stir. Place it over medium-low heat.
2. Cook for 5 minutes, making sure to keep stirring the mixture. Transfer to a serving bowl. Serve and enjoy!

Nutrition:

- **Calories:** 123
- **Fat:** 1.3g
- **Carbohydrates:**23g
- **Protein:** 4g

44. Simple Granola Platter

Preparation time: 5 minutes

Cooking time: 25 minutes.

Servings: 4

Ingredients:

- 1-ounce porridge oats
- 2 teaspoons of maple syrup
- Cooking spray as needed
- 4 medium bananas
- 5-ounce fresh fruit salad, such as strawberries, blueberries, and raspberries
- ¼ ounce pumpkin seeds
- ¼ ounce sunflower seeds
- ¼ ounce dry Chia seeds
- ¼ ounce desiccated coconut

Directions:

1. Preheat your oven to 300°F. Prepare a baking tray then line it with baking paper. Take a large bowl and add oats, maple syrup, and seeds.
2. Spread mix on a baking tray. Spray coconut oil on top and bake for 20 minutes, making sure to keep stirring it from time to time.
3. Sprinkle coconut after the first 15 minutes. Remove from oven and let it cool. Take a bowl and layer sliced bananas. Spread the cooled granola mix on top and serve with a topping of berries. Enjoy!

Nutrition:

- **Calories:** 446
- **Fat:** 29g
- **Carbohydrates:** 37g
- **Protein:** 13g

45. Buffalo Cashew

Preparation time: 10 minutes.

Cooking time: 55 minutes.

Servings: 4

Ingredients:

- 2 cups raw cashews
- ¾ cup red hot sauce
- 1/3 cup avocado oil
- ½ teaspoon garlic powder
- ¼ teaspoon turmeric

Directions:

1. Take a bowl and mix wet ingredients in a bowl and stir in seasoning. Add cashews to the bowl and mix. Soak cashews in hot sauce mix for 2–4 hours.
2. Preheat your oven to 325°F. Spread cashews onto the baking sheet. Bake for 35–55 minutes, turning after every 10–15 minutes. Let them cool and serve!

Nutrition:

- **Calories:** 268
- **Fat:** 16g
- **Carbohydrates:** 20g
- **Protein:** 14g

46. Apple and Cinnamon Oatmeal

Preparation time: 10 minutes.

Cooking time: 10 minutes.

Servings: 2

Ingredients:

- 1 ¼ cups apple cider
- 1 apple, peeled, cored, and chopped
- 2/3 cup rolled oats
- 1 teaspoon ground cinnamon
- 1 tablespoon pure maple syrup

Directions:

1. Take a medium-sized saucepan, bring apple cider to a boil over medium-high heat. Stir in apples, oats, and cinnamon.
2. Bring cereal to a boil and lower heat, simmer for 3–4 minutes until thickened. Spoon between two bowls and serve with maple syrup, enjoy!

Nutrition:

- **Calories:** 339
- **Fat:** 14g
- **Carbohydrates:** 40g
- **Protein:** 8g

47. Sweet Potato Toast with Blueberries

Preparation time: 15 minutes.

Cooking time: 30 minutes.

Servings: 10 slices.

Ingredients:

- 1 large sweet potato, rinsed and cut into 10 slices
- 20 blueberries
- 2 tablespoons almond butter

Directions:

1. Warm your oven to 350°F. Put a wire rack on your baking sheet. Arrange the sweet potato slices on the wire rack, then cook in the preheated oven for 15 or until soft.
2. Flip the sweet potato slices every 5 minutes to make sure evenly cooked. Then toast immediately or store in the refrigerator.
3. To make the sweet potato toast, put the cooked sweet potato slices in a toaster in batches and toast over medium for 15 minutes or until crispy and

golden brown. Serve the toast with blueberries and almond butter.

Nutrition:

- **Calories:** 374
- **Fat:** 18.1g
- **Carbs:** 47.2g
- **Protein:** 10.5g

48. Almond Butter Cookies

Preparation time: 45 minutes.

Cooking time: 12 minutes.

Servings: 10

Ingredients:

- 3/4 cup all-purpose flour
- 1/2 teaspoon baking soda
- 1/4 teaspoon kosher salt
- 1 flax egg
- 1/4 cup coconut oil
- 2 tablespoons almond milk
- 1/2 cup brown sugar
- 1/2 cup almond butter
- 1/2 teaspoon ground cinnamon
- 1/2 teaspoon vanilla

Directions:

1. Mix the flour, baking soda plus salt in a mixing bowl. In another bowl, combine the flax egg, coconut oil, almond milk, sugar, almond butter, cinnamon, and vanilla. Stir the wet batter into the dry ingredients and stir until well combined.
2. Place the batter in your refrigerator for about 30 minutes. Shape the batter into small cookies and arrange them on a parchment-lined cookie pan.
3. Bake at 350°F within 12 minutes in a preheated oven. Move the pan to the wire rack to cool at room temperature. Bon appétit!

Nutrition:

- **Calories:** 197
- **Fat:** 15.8g
- **Carbs:** 12.5g
- **Protein:** 2.1g

49. Fluffy Coconut Blondies with Raisins

Preparation time: 15 minutes.

Cooking time: 25 minutes.

Servings: 9

Ingredients:

- 1 cup coconut flour
- 1 cup all-purpose flour
- 1/2 teaspoon baking powder
- 1/4 teaspoon salt
- 1 cup desiccated coconut, unsweetened
- 3/4 cup vegan butter, softened
- 1(½) cups brown sugar
- 3 tablespoons applesauce
- 1/2 teaspoon vanilla extract
- 1/2 teaspoon ground anise
- 1 cup raisins, soaked for 15 minutes

Directions:

1. Warm your oven to 350°F. Brush a baking pan with nonstick cooking oil.
2. Thoroughly combine the flour, baking powder, salt, and coconut. In another bowl, mix the butter, sugar, applesauce, vanilla, and anise. Stir the butter mixture into the dry ingredients; stir to combine well.
3. Fold in the raisins. Press the batter into the baking pan. Bake within 25 minutes or until it is set in the middle. Place the cake on a wire rack to cool slightly. Bon appétit!

Nutrition:

- **Calories:** 365
- **Fat:** 18.5
- **Carbs:** 49g
- **Protein:** 2.1g

50. Jasmine Rice Pudding with Dried Apricots

Preparation time: 15 minutes.

Cooking time: 0 minutes.

Servings: 4

Ingredients:

- 1 cup jasmine rice, rinsed
- 1 cup water
- 1 cup almond milk
- 1/2 cup brown sugar
- A pinch of salt
- A pinch of grated nutmeg
- 1/2 cup dried apricots, chopped
- 1/4 teaspoon cinnamon powder
- 1 teaspoon vanilla extract

Directions:

1. Put the rice plus water into a saucepan. Cover your saucepan, then boil the water. Adjust the heat to low; simmer for another 10 minutes until all the water is absorbed.
2. Then add the remaining ingredients and stir to combine. Let it simmer for 10 minutes more or until the pudding has thickened. Bon appétit!

Nutrition:

- **Calories:** 300
- **Fat:** 2.2g
- **Carbs:** 63.6g
- **Protein:** 5.6g

51.Banana Blueberry Bread

Preparation time: 15 minutes.

Cooking time: 35 minutes.

Servings: 8

Ingredients:

- 3 tablespoons lemon juice
- 4 bananas
- ½ cup agave nectar
- ½ cup vegan milk
- 1(¾) cup all-purpose flour
- 1 teaspoon baking soda
- 1 teaspoon baking powder
- 1 teaspoon salt
- 2 cups blueberries

Directions:

1. Warm your oven to 350°F. Mix the dry ingredients in a large bowl and your wet ingredients in a different, smaller bowl. Make sure to mash up the bananas well.
2. Stir the ingredients together in the large bowl, making sure to assimilate the ingredients together completely.
3. Add the blueberries last and then pour the mixture into a bread pan. Allow the bread to bake for 50 minutes, and enjoy.

Nutrition:

- **Calories:** 155
- **Carbs:** 31g
- **Fat:** 2g
- **Protein:** 5g

52. Pecan Pie Pudding

Preparation time: 5 minutes.

Cooking time: 0 minutes.

Servings: 1

Ingredients:

- ¾ cup plain full-fat Greek yogurt
- ½ scoop low-carb vanilla protein powder
- 4 tablespoons chopped pecans
- 2 tablespoons sugar-free syrup

Directions:

1. Mix the Greek yogurt plus protein powder in a small bowl until smooth and creamy. Top with the chopped pecans and syrup.

Nutrition:

- **Calories:** 381
- **Fat:** 21g
- **Protein:** 32g
- **Carbs:** 16g

53. Chocolate Avocado Pudding

Preparation time: 5 minutes.

Cooking time: 0 minutes.

Servings: 1

Ingredients:

- 1 avocado, halved
- 1/3 cup full-fat coconut milk
- 1 teaspoon vanilla extract
- 2 tablespoons unsweetened cocoa powder
- 5 or 6 drops liquid stevia

Directions:

1. Combine all the ingredients in a high-powered blender or food processor and blend until smooth. Serve immediately.

Nutrition:

- **Calories:** 555
- **Fat:** 47g
- **Protein:** 7g
- **Carbs:** 26g

54. Overnight Oats on the Go

Preparation time: 5 minutes.

Cooking time: 5 minutes or overnight.

Servings: 1 serving.

Ingredients:

Basic overnight oats:

- ½ cup rolled oats, or quinoa flakes for gluten-free
- 1 tablespoon ground flaxseed, or chia seeds, or hemp hearts
- 1 tablespoon maple syrup, or coconut sugar (optional)
- ¼ teaspoon ground cinnamon (optional)

Topping options:

- 1 apple, chopped, and 1 tablespoon walnuts
- 2 tablespoons dried cranberries and 1 tablespoon pumpkin seeds
- 1 pear, chopped, and 1 tablespoon cashews
- 1 cup sliced grapes and 1 tablespoon sunflower seeds
- 1 banana, sliced, and 1 tablespoon peanut butter

- 2 tablespoons raisins and 1 tablespoon hazelnuts
- 1 cup berries and 1 tablespoon unsweetened coconut flakes

Directions:

1. Mix the oats, flax, maple syrup, and cinnamon (if using) in a bowl or to-go container (a travel mug or short thermos works beautifully).
2. Pour enough cool water over the oats to submerge them and stir to combine. Leave to soak for a minimum of half an hour, or overnight.
3. Add your choice of toppings.

Nutrition:

- **Calories:** 244
- **Total fat:** 6g
- **Carbs:** 30g
- **Fiber:** 6g
- **Protein:** 7g

55. Lovely Baby Potatoes

Preparation time: 10 minutes.

Cooking time: 35 minutes.

Servings: 4

Ingredients:

- 2 pounds new yellow potatoes, scrubbed and cut into wedges
- 2 tablespoons extra-virgin olive oil
- 2 teaspoons fresh rosemary, chopped
- 1 teaspoon garlic powder
- ½ teaspoon freshly ground black pepper and sunflower seeds

Directions:

1. Preheat your oven to 400°F. Line baking sheet with aluminum foil and set aside. Take a large bowl and add potatoes, olive oil, garlic, rosemary, sea sunflower seeds, and pepper.
2. Spread potatoes in a single layer on a baking sheet and bake for 35 minutes. Serve and enjoy!

Nutrition:

- **Calories:** 225
- **Fat:** 7g
- **Carbohydrates:** 37g
- **Protein:** 5g

56. Roasted Veg with Creamy Avocado Dip

Preparation time: 10 minutes.

Cooking time: 30 minutes.

Servings: 2

Ingredients:

For the avocado dip:

- 1 avocado
- 1 tablespoon apple cider vinegar
- ¼ to ½ cup of water
- 2 tablespoons nutritional yeast
- 1 teaspoon dried dill/1 tablespoon fresh dill
- Pinch sea salt

For the roasted veg:

- 1 small sweet potato, peeled and cubed
- 2 small beets, peeled and cubed
- 2 small carrots, peeled and cubed
- 1 teaspoon of sea salt
- 1 teaspoon dried oregano
- ¼ teaspoon cayenne pepper
- Pinch freshly ground black pepper

Directions:

1. **To make the avocado dip:** In a blender, purée the avocado with the other dip ingredients, using just enough water to get a smooth, creamy texture.
2. Alternatively, you can mash the avocado thoroughly in a large bowl and then stir in the rest of the dip ingredients.
3. **To make the roasted veg:** Preheat the oven to 350°F. Put the sweet potato, beets, and carrots in a large pot with a small amount of water, and bring to a boil over high heat.
4. Boil for 15 minutes until they're just barely soft, then drain. Sprinkle the salt, oregano, cayenne, and pepper over them and stir gently to combine. (Use more or less cayenne depending on your taste).
5. Spread the vegetables on a large baking sheet and roast them in the oven for 10 to 15 minutes until they've browned around the edges. Serve the veg with the avocado dip on the side.

Nutrition:

- **Calories:** 335
- **Fat:** 12g
- **Carbs:** 51g
- **Protein:** 11g

57. Baked Banana French Toast with Raspberry Syrup

Preparation time: 10 minutes.

Cooking time: 30 minutes.

Servings: 8 slices

Ingredients:

For the French toast:

- 1 banana
- 1 cup of coconut milk
- 1 teaspoon pure vanilla extract
- ¼ teaspoon ground nutmeg
- ½ teaspoon ground cinnamon
- 1½ teaspoons arrowroot powder or flour
- Pinch sea salt
- 8 slices whole-grain bread

For the raspberry syrup:

- 1 cup raspberries/other berries
- 2 tablespoons water, or pure fruit juice
- 1 to 2 tablespoons maple syrup or coconut sugar (optional)

Directions:

1. For the French toast, preheat the oven to 350°F. In a shallow bowl, purée or mash the banana well. Mix in coconut milk, vanilla, nutmeg, cinnamon, arrowroot, and salt.
2. Dip the slices of bread in the banana mixture and then lay them out in a 13-by-9-inch baking dish. They should cover the bottom of the dish and overlap slightly but shouldn't be stacked on top of each other.
3. Pour any leftover banana mixture over the bread, and put the dish in the oven—Bake within 30 minutes, or until the tops are lightly browned. Serve topped with raspberry syrup.
4. **To make the raspberry syrup:** Heat the raspberries in a small pot with the water and the maple syrup (if using) on medium heat.Leave to simmer, stirring

occasionally, and breaking up the berries for 15 to 20 minutes until the liquid has reduced.

Nutrition:

- **Calories:** 166
- **Fat:** 7g
- **Carbs:** 23g
- **Protein:** 5g

58. Walnut, Coconut and Oat Granola

Preparation time: 15 minutes.

Cooking time: 1 hour and 40 minutes.

Servings: 4

Ingredients:

- 1 cup chopped walnuts
- 1 cup unsweetened, shredded coconut
- 2 cups rolled oats
- 1 teaspoon ground cinnamon
- 2 tablespoons hemp seeds
- 2 tablespoons ground flaxseeds
- 2 tablespoons chia seeds
- ¾ teaspoon salt (optional)
- ¼ cup maple syrup
- ¼ cup water
- 1 teaspoon vanilla extract
- ½ cup dried cranberries

Directions:

1. Preheat the oven to 250°F (120°C). Line a baking sheet with parchment paper.
2. Mix the walnuts, coconut, rolled oats, cinnamon, hemp seeds, flaxseeds, chia seeds, and salt (if desired) into a bowl.
3. Combine the maple syrup and water in a saucepan. Bring to a boil over medium heat, then pour in the bowl of walnut mixture.
4. Add the vanilla extract to the bowl of the mixture. Stir to mix well. Pour the mixture into the baking sheet, then level with a spatula so the mixture coats the bottom evenly.
5. Place the baking sheet in the preheated oven and bake for 90 minutes or until browned and crispy. Stir the mixture every 15 minutes.
6. Remove the baking sheet from the oven. Allow to cool for 10 minutes, then serve with dried cranberries on top.

Nutrition:

- **Calories:** 1870
- **Fat:** 115.8g
- **Carbs:** 238.0g
- **Protein:** 59.8g
- **Fiber:** 68.9g

59. Banana Bread

Preparation time: 1 hour and 5 minutes.

Cooking time: 10 minutes.

Servings: 12

Ingredients:

- 3 bananas, ripe
- 1/3 cup applesauce, unsweetened
- ¼ cup almond milk
- 1 teaspoon vanilla extract
- 1¾ cup whole wheat flour
- 1/3 cup coconut sugar
- 2 teaspoons baking powder
- ½ teaspoon baking soda
- 1/3 cup chopped walnuts
- ¼ teaspoon salt

Directions:

1. Preheat the oven to 350°F. Prepare a 9-inch loaf pan lined using parchment paper. Mash your bananas in a medium bowl until smooth. Add applesauce, vanilla, and almond milk and mix well.
2. Add all the rest ingredients. Stir, but do not over-process. Pour batter into loaf pan. Use a spatula to smooth the top. Bake for 50 to 55 minutes. Serve.

Nutrition:

- **Calories:** 120
- **Fat:** 0.5g
- **Protein:** 2.5g
- **Carbs:** 27g

60. Toast with Cannellini Beans and Pesto

Preparation time: 5 minutes.

Cooking time: 0 minutes.

Servings: 1

Ingredients:

- 1 slice whole-wheat bread (toasted)
- 1/3 cup canned cannellini beans (no-salt added)
- 1 pinch garlic powder
- ½ teaspoon basil pesto
- 2 tablespoons tomato (chopped)

Directions:

1. Start by rinsing and draining the canned cannellini beans. Keep aside. Take the toasted slice and place it on a plate.
2. Take a small mixing bowl and add the beans, tomatoes, and garlic powder. Mix well. Place the prepared beans and the tomato mixture on the toast and top with pesto. Serve.

Nutrition:

- **Calories:** 366
- **Carbs:** 49g
- **Fat:** 12g
- **Protein:** 21g

In the same series you can find:

PLANT BASED DIET: THE BENEFITS OF A VEGETARIAN DIET

PLANT BASED DIET COOKBOOK: RECIPES FOR YOUR LUNCH

PLANT BASED DIET COOKBOOK: RECIPES FOR YOUR DINNER

PLANT BASED DIET COOKBOOK: RECIPES FOR YOUR SALADS

PLANT BASED DIET COOKBOOK: RECIPES FOR YOUR DESSERTS

PLANT BASED DIET COOKBOOK: SUPERFOODS RECIPES

PLANT BASED DIET COOKBOOK: ALKALINE FOODS RECIPES

PLANT BASED DIET COOKBOOK: RECIPES FOR YOUR JUICES&SMOOTHIES

CPSIA information can be obtained
at www.ICGtesting.com
Printed in the USA
BVHW051025110821
614178BV00002B/124